Built
FOR THE BATTLE

EVANGELIST
O'KEIYA DINNALL

BUILT FOR THE BATTLE

Please direct all copyright inquiries to:

B.O.Y. Publications, Inc.
c/o Author Copyrights
P.O. Box 262
Lowell, NC 28098
betonyourselfent.com

Paperback ISBN: 978-1-955605-69-4

Cover and Interior Design: B.O.Y. Enterprises, Inc.
Contributing Editor: Sucora Williams Anderson

Printed in the United States.

Dedication

This book is dedicated to With My Sisters Inc. To every sister on the team, I appreciate you.

Acknowledgements

I would like to express my deepest appreciation to Sucora Anderson, a gifted freelance writer based in Wilmington, NC. Her invaluable assistance in typing and editing this book has been instrumental in bringing it to fruition.

Sucora, with her lifelong passion for writing and her remarkable ability to communicate, has not only contributed her expertise but also her heart to this project. Her contributions to local and regional publications, her love for people, and her joy in telling their stories are a testament to her dedication and love for her craft.

As a woman of faith, Sucora lives by the mantra, "I can do all things through Christ who gives me strength." This strength and faith have been a guiding light throughout the process of creating this book.

Thank you so much my friend

To the love of my life,

For 27 remarkable years, you have been my constant source of strength and inspiration. Your unwavering faith in me has been the driving force behind every word I've penned in this devotional book.

Your encouragement has been my guiding light in moments of doubt, and your gentle push has propelled me to transcend boundaries I never thought possible. Your prayers have been my shield, protecting me from despair and guiding me towards hope.

Thank you for not giving up on me, for seeing the potential in me even when I failed to see it in myself. Your belief in me has made this journey not just possible, but profoundly meaningful.

With all my heart, I dedicate this book to you. May it serve as a testament to our shared faith, our enduring love, and the extraordinary journey we've embarked upon together.

I am yours forever, Fray Dinnall.

Table of Contents

It's Time to Get Up and Move

I t is time to get up and move from the place you have been for so long. Sometimes things happen in our lives, and we get stuck. This can happen due to trauma, tragedy, or just the issues of life. We get in a place and sometimes it is hard to bounce back. But today is your day that you shall come unstuck. In Deuteronomy 2: God tells Mosses that they have been in a place too long and it is time to move. It is time to change your direction. It is time to stop going around the same mountain. Today is the day to climb over the mountain to get to your next place—to your best. God has a place of promise for us. He has a blessing for us, but we have got to go forward and possess the land. We have to first believe that God wants the best for us. Then we have to mentally see ourselves in that place. We have to commit to doing the work and then we must go forward to posses the land— the promise God has for us. We must let God heal our mind, body, spirit and soul. We cannot live in the past and possess the future God has for us. Sometimes I know it seems life can hit us so hard that it feels that we can not recover. But we serve a mighty God. He knows everything we go through. He knows every hurt and every pain. We must trust Him and the plan He has to prosper us and give us an expected end. Let him pull you out of the stuck place. Let Him make you over. If you are reading this book, I want you to get excited for what He has in store for you. He is not finished with you yet. God is the potter, and we are the lump of clay in His hands.

"Oh Israel, can I not do to you as this potter has done to his clay? As the clay is in the potter's hand, so are you in my hand." **-Jeremiah 18:6**

Reflection

The Lord Knows

Dear Heavenly Father, I ask that you touch and heal our hearts today. Let the love of God overtake us today. Lord today we give you our brokenness to make us whole again. Lord touch us like never before. Give us beauty for ashes—In Jesus' name.

"The Lord is close to the brokenhearted and saves those who are crushed in spirit." **-Psalm 34:18**

In the Psalm, it seems clear that those who are going through trails are the ones who are crushed in spirit. In light of the promises made by the Psalmist David, for those who take refuge in the Lord, we can assume that he is talking about those who find trouble, not because of their unrighteousness, but because there is trouble in this world. He promises that "The righteous person may have many troubles. But the Lord delivers him from them all."

We must remember that the Lord knows and feels everything we go through. And He wants to heal our hearts and put us back together when we are broken. The Lord loves us so much and He is always right there to be a life saver for us. This scripture reminds us that he is close to the brokenhearted. In His word, He promised that He will never leave us or forsake us. In our darkest times he is that bright light. When we cry, he catches our tears in a bottle.

We are going to go through things in our life that feel just like our heart is being crushed and broken. The good news is that God cares for us. He is always going to be right by our side. The word tells us that, "Weeping may endure for a moment, but Joy comes in the morning." Give God your brokenness and watch Him do a new thing in your life.

I remember when I lost my grandma, oh that was the hardest day in my life. It felt just like I had lost my best friend. It seemed like it was so hard to bear the grief. My heart felt empty and shattered. I cried for days, but guess what, Jesus was with me every step of the way. I cried out to the Lord, and He heard my cry. Jesus filled that place in my heart. He gave me peace and he comforted me. Today take time to cry out to the Lord and let him heal your broken heart and fill that place in your heart where you are grieving.

Do not give up on God, because He will never give up on you. Rejoice today because the Lord is close to us every day—whether you feel Him or not. He is there. Our Lord and savior will never fail us. Trust Him today and take Him at His word. He is Abba—our father. He is as close to us as the air we breathe. The thoughts and plans that God has for are amazing.

Remember all the heartaches, rejection and brokenness we have felt or may still be feeling, have come to make us stronger. "Oh, taste and see that the Lord is good." Be encouraged today. Let the love of God put a smile on your face. For He is with you.

It is time. This is the moment that we need to surrender our brokenness, rejection, tears, heartache, fear and insecurities to Him.

"So let us come boldly to the throne of our gracious God. There we will receive his mercy and we will find grace to help us when we need it most." **-Hebrews 4:16 NLT**

Reflection

The Moment of Surrender

We all have a spiritual birthday—a set time when all that we have been through finally culminates in that moment of revelation, when we understand the purpose for which we have been created. That moment is predestined by God. Jerimiah 29:11 confirms this truth, *"For I know the thoughts that I think toward you, saith the LORD, thoughts of peace, and not of evil, to give you an expected end."* The struggles, tragedies, trauma, rejections, mistakes, disappointments, and failures- refine us and prepare us for the expected end. There is purpose in what you have been through. Not everything we have been through is good, but we can finally be good, if we give God the glory and declare that *"For all things work together for good for those that love the Lord, and diligently seek after Him."* It is not all good, but God can make it work for our good.

The Lord sees not only who we are now, but who we can become according to His plans. Our past---- the traumas we have endured, the challenges we have faced and fought to overcome, do not define our future nor limit our possibilities of who can be, or what we can achieve or accomplish. The challenges come to shape us and to mold us for the purpose for which God has predestined. But only when we surrender it all to Him- the tragedies, trauma, rejections, mistakes, disappointments and failures-can we finally become free to be all that He says we can be. God can use it all for our good and He does…. "For all things work together for good for those who love Him."

At age 40, I, Evangelist O'Keiya Dinnall, founder and executive director of the non-profit, "With Our Sisters," had that moment of surrender when I realized that God had predestined me for an expected purpose. And nothing in my past limited or excluded me from God's plan for my life.

As a young woman growing up, I felt rejected by my peers and was often picked on and made fun of. I internalized the opinion of others and adopted it as my own self-identity. "Something must be wrong with me." "If only I wasn't different." But thank God He did not give up on me! I surrendered my emotions to the Lord and by His grace, I changed the narrative. I made a conscious decision to be the woman that God called me to be. Who says you can't wear white after Labor Day?

For every little girl, or young woman who has ever felt this way, or young man who has felt different or "not good enough, this word is for you. To help you along on your journey of hearing God's voice and accepting his plan for your life. To feel his love and know that you have been "fearfully and wonderfully made."

> *"For it was You who created my inward parts; you knit me together in my mother's womb. I will praise you because I have been fearfully and wonderfully made."* -**Psalms 139:13-14**

Reflection

Time to Rest

The dictionary defines rest as: "peace of mind or spirit. Freedom from activity and labor.

Rest is required on this journey called life. Yes, I know we go to bed at night and sleep. But that is not rest. A lot of the time, we have so much on our minds that we cannot rest. That is when we need to give it to God. He says in His word to "give him all our burdens and our worriers so that we can have rest." Mathew 11:28-30 says, "Come to me, all you who are weary and burdened, and I will give you rest. Take my yoke upon you and learn from me, for I am gentle and humble in heart, and you will find rest for your souls. For my yoke is easy and my burden is light." God wants us to get rest so that we can be replenished and restored. He does not want us walking around weighed down by the troubles of life. He is our rock and our strong tower. He is our savior and provider.

When you go to bed at night, ask God to let you enter a place of rest. Let him lay you down by the still waters. Trust God that while you are resting, He is taking care of all your needs. Resting is also part of self-care and self-love. In order to be the best, you, you have to let your mind, body and soul rest. It is okay to take a day off from the world. Rest in the arms of Jesus. Let the Lord pour out His love on you. Remember, Jesus went to sleep on the boat, and He was resting, even while the storm was raging, He was able to rest. He then got up and spoke "Peace be still". When the storms come into our lives, remember you can have peace and rest. Just as long as you have Jesus. He is your anchor. He is your safety net. Give yourself permission to rest. We are not called to be superheroes. We are called to be God's children and to let Him take care of us. So today cast all your worries and cares to Jesus. Rest in Him. Let Him lead and guide you every step of the way. Let your mid be a peace knowing that God has got everything you need. Even when it comes to food, clothes, shelter and so many other things. Gods got it. And He's got you. Father today help us to learn to lean and depend on you. Father as we lay down, we give you all our burdens. God take us to a place of rest for our mind, body and soul. In Jesus name, Amen!

*"But now the Lord my God has given me rest on every side. There is neither adversary nor misfortune." ***-1 Kings 5:4**

Reflection

Who Says You Can't Wear White After Labor Day?

"Just Be You"

We spend so much time trying to fit in with everyone one else that often we forget that it is okay not to fit in. In fact, we were created not to fit. God made each one of us uniquely individual. Which means, we are free to be different according to His purpose for us.

"I will praise thee for I am fearfully and wonderfully made; marvelous are thy works; and that my soul knoweth right well." -Psalm 139:14

Every day, we should strive to be who He created us to be. No one can be you...only you can be you. We waste so much time comparing ourselves to others. We often try to the point of anguish to "fit-in," or to be accepted or gain approval. We wait for others to celebrate us and to validate our achievements, our gifts our style, or talent and on and on. This is a distraction. A tool that Satan uses to keep up bound up and tethered to his lies. He is successful, only if we allow him to have victory over us.

Push back on his lies and learn to celebrate yourself. In fact, if no one else celebrates you, you celebrate you. Stand in the mirror and practice telling yourself that you are enough because the God who created you, is enough—we are enough because He is enough. Learn to love, accept, and celebrate you— His unique creation. We are not who others say we are or who they try to tell us that we must be. In fact, what others say and declare over us is not nearly as important as who God says we are and what He declares over us. God says that we are, *"The apple of His eye,"* (Deuteronomy 32.10 NIV) and *"A peculiar treasure,"* (Exodus 19:5-8) KJV.

"Now therefore, If ye will obey my voice indeed, and keep my covenant then ye shall be a peculiar treasure unto me above all people" -**Exodus 19:5-8 KJV**

We are not our hair, or our makeup, or our clothes, but again we are, *"fearfully and wonderfully made."* We should enjoy celebrating who we are and what makes us unique. We should express our own individual personalities and uniqueness. As long as it is okay with God, it is okay for us.

We must learn to love and accept ourselves as we are. And that encompasses accepting our hair, our bodies, our unique talents, and gifts. Be who God created you to be. Stop compromising to fit into someone else's opinion or idea of who you should be. Or someone else's opinion of what you should look like or sound like or dress like for that matter.

Don't worry about what other people are going to say. Or what will be said if you show up in all white in December. The opinion of others can paralyze us if we let it. Be mindful to stop and listen to your inner voice…your inner self. Who do you say you are. And do you feel okay with who you are.

Learn to love yourself not because of what others say about you, but in spite of what others say about you. Like you enough for you. And be who God says you are, *"The apple of His eye," "A peculiar treasure."*

So, if you like pink, go ahead and wear it. And if you feel like it—wear that white suit after Labor Day. Go ahead, express yourself!

It's time for A Push in The Spirit.

Reflection

A Push in the Spirit

It's Time to Answer the Call

Philippians 3:14: *"I press on to reach the end of the race and receive the heavenly prize for which God, through Christ Jesus, is calling us."*

Do we really believe God and His Word? We waste so much time waiting on validation from others to tell us that we can do what God has already called us to do. It's time to "level up" and answer the call.

Track runners in a competition start out with the baton. The goal is to run the first leg and then pass the baton to the next runner. Sometimes the baton does get dropped. What happens then? Do you pick up the baton and keep running or do you just stand there and marvel at it. Why do we do this? God's word hasn't changed neither has His call on your life or His plans for your life. The finish line is in sight, but in order to get to it, we must pick up the baton and run. Press toward the finish line. Press toward the mark. It's time to bust a move.

Forget about people and what they think or what they say. It doesn't really matter. Stop making excuses. If we will just take the first step, God will show us the next step and the next step. We need to repent when we are not following God's plan. Pressing toward your call will require a change in our mindsets. We will never be more or accomplish more than we believe by faith that we can. God has placed the baton in our hand. The pressure is on us to run or to just stand there looking at it. We are perfectly positioned for God to move and for Him to produce a miracle. But to make it to the finish line, it is going to require a press. And guess what, the working power of the holy ghost is present to aid us in the race.

The experiences we have in life come to push us and to strengthen our faith. We must learn to take God at His word and commit our ways to Him. To stop making excuses or elevating the problems or the challenges that hold us back. It is time to stop telling God what we think or what we feel. Or even what we believe of what people have told us about ourselves. Instead, our mindset should be, that Father, not my will but yours be done. Father, I refuse to quit and give up. I refuse to let others hold me back or to respond to their actions or what they say about me. I choose to hear from you Lord. I choose to keep running. I choose to rise and shine today knowing that the Glory of the Lord is upon me and that I can do all things through Him who gives me strength. I choose to look up to the hills from where my help comes. I choose to rise, elevate and exhort the Lord my God. I choose today to shine bright for Him. I chose today to walk in my gifts and to become obedient to His instruction. I chose to believe that I am who He says I am. I chose today to be who He says I can be. I chose today to have what He says I can have. I chose today to keep running. I chose today to bust-a-move.

Time is too precious to waste. Life is just a vapor.

Reflection

Just a Vapor

Life is nothing but a vapor. In one blink, it can be over. An accident, one trauma, one injury, can change your life in a second. So, you must take hold and embrace each day and commit to living it to the fullest as though it could be your last.

Each day is a day of grace and mercy. You cannot turn back the hands of time. You cannot get a do over. But what you can do is to move forward. Learn from yesterday and try not to make the same mistakes. You must live with a made-up mind that even if something feels like a setback, let that be the fuel to launch you forward. Let the hurt and the pain propel you to your next level.

Your happiness and joy await. We were born with a light inside of us. A light that can shine so brightly if we choose to turn it on. The seasons of our life change just like the falling leaves of fall. There is a time of shedding. In the winter, things wither and die. Sometimes things must die in our lives—old habits, old mind-sets, old issues, and attitudes for the Holy Spirit to transition you into your new season. Use your fall and winter to prepare for your spring—your new birth. Your season to shine. Your season to live.

It is up to you how you live your life. But just know that greatness awaits. It is only a step away. One foot forward can change your life. One decision. Just know that your dreams, your ideas matter. Someone needs you to come alive and live. Through death Jesus rose with all power. If you feel like you are in a dead season, just know that you are about to rise. Keep the faith, do not lose hope. Because in the darkest moments, you will find yourself as Jesus was in the tomb. I believe it was a dark cold place. But I also believe that it was in those moments that He found His strength concerning death and rose.

He rose with all power in His hands. He defeated death and so will you. You will find the strength to rise out of your tomb. What was sent to crush you is the thing God will use to make you. It is sharpening your spiritual muscles and building your endurance. Seize the day— seize this moment. "To seize the day" means to make the most of the present moment. To make each day count and to get the most out of your day.

When you wake up every morning, give praise and thanks to the Lord Almighty that you made it through the night. *"This is the day that the Lord has made, let us rejoice and be glad in in." (Psalm 11:8-24)* The night is over; the dawn is here. Take deep breaths, God is with you and the Holy spirit goes before you. Put a smile on your face and a song in your heart. The way is made, and your steps are ordered! The only person that can stop you now is you.

It doesn't matter what anyone else thinks. All that matters is what you think and what you believe about yourself. Look in a mirror and tell yourself that you are going to make it. That you have what it takes to make an impact through the Lord. Once you break out of the tomb—dark place, to spread your wings and soar. Remember, a butterfly cannot turn back into a caterpillar once its transformation has taken place. So, no matter what comes, don't go back to that dark place. Keep your head up and your wings open. God will call you even when you don't feel equipped. In your weakness is when he can use you because it will be him that you rely on and not yourself. Pray this prayer— Dear Heavenly Father, I ask you to open my eyes that I may see what you see. Father, help me to move forward in the things that you have called me to do. Let the wind of God blow on me today. Giving me supernatural energy to get everything you have for me to accomplish on this day. Lord, forgive me for where I have been slack. Let me be proactive. I shall walk this day knowing that I have purpose and work to do for the Kingdom. Amen.

"But those who hope in the Lord will renew their strength. they will soar on wings like eagles they will run and not grow weary they will walk and not be faint." **-Isaiah 40:31 (NLT)**

Reflection

Keep Going

Why do we doubt God when we already know he tells the sun when to rise, the wind when to blow and the ocean how far out to go and the moon when to come out. He set the stars in the sky and created the earth simply by the authority of His word. He is the almighty creator of heaven and the earth. Yet, sometimes, we doubt what God can do. Surely the God of creation, has dominion over you and your circumstances.

We must learn to trust God in the midst of our storms and to keep going. God has promised in His word that "When you pass through the waters, I will be with you. And through the rivers, they will not overtake you. When you walk through the fire, you will not be scorched, and the flames will not overtake you." *(Isaiah 43:2)*

God is the strength we need—His strength is made perfect in our weakness. So, when we're going through, we must press through it. We have to pull up our bootstraps my sisters, dry up our tears and press on past our situation.

It is easy to give up. But to keep going, it will require faith. We must trust Him and believe His word and His promises. Moving past the circumstances will also require us to move past comfortable places. We often become comfortable in our circumstances. However, to experience the fullness of what he has for us, we have to get off the shore and move out into the deep. We must pass through the troubled waters to get to the other side. Remaining on the shore requires no risk. But God has more for us. To possess His promises will require us to press through the troubled waters to get to the other side. Remember, we already have the victory through the promises in His word. He says, "the battle is not ours, but belongs to the Lord." *(2 Chronicles 20:15)* He has promised to pull us through the dark places. He is the light. We must remain determined to press toward the light.

Weeping may endure for a night, but joy comes in the morning. March on toward the light and keep looking to the one who is the source of our strength. He is the strength we need to keep going. His love and His promise will never fail.

"I look up to the mountains does my help come from there. My help comes for the Lord who made heaven and earth."
-**Psalms 121:1-2 (NLT)**

Reflection

Stay In Position

A line of formation once utilized by military forces in a battle was considered a fundamental battle tactic because it enabled forces to deploy the maximum amount of firepower in one direction at once.

For the believer today dealing with challenges and the attacks of the enemy which are deployed to cause doubt and unbelief in the word of God, requires us to stay in position, in other words, to remain in formation, with our weapons of war—prayer, fasting and praise, fully engaged and aimed directly at the devil our enemy.

Daniel stayed in position in Chapter 10. He continued to pray and fast for twenty-one days until the answers which had been held up were revealed to him. He believed that God was own his side and by faith, victory. We must go out every day believing that God is on our side and that he has already fought our battles. Be diligent and steadfast in declaring that your miracle has already been released. He has everything worked out. We must, however, declare the word of the lord over our circumstances. We must declare that our answers are here, and that our miracle is now. He has promised to give us a future and hope. Stand firm in formation and let your faith cancel out your doubt.

Understanding in the process that the "weight" of our circumstance and the "wait of the victory will require us to press. But allowing God to have his way in us to do his perfect work is developing us into the kingdom women He has called us to be. As physical weights build our muscles and endurance in the natural, spiritual weights do the same thing for our spirit man. It develops our spiritual muscles and builds our faith and endurance. Be confident in the Lord, that the weight and the wait are not going to break you, but they will make you. Allow the seeds of your faith to take root. Be confident that Victory is in your view. Stand firm, hold your position, and remain in formation. He will not fail you. God has you.

"Therefore, I tell you, whatever you ask for in prayer, believe that you have received it, and it will be yours."

Reflection

Know Who You Belong To

David said in Psalm 23: *"The Lord is my shepherd; I shall not want. He maketh me to lie down in green pastures: he leadeth me beside the still waters. He restoreth my soul: he leadeth me in the paths of righteousness for his name's sake. Yea, though I walk through the valley of the shadow of death, I will fear no evil: for thou art with me; thy rod and thy staff they comfort me. Thou preparest a table before me in the presence of mine enemies: thou anointest my head with oil; my cup runneth over. Surely goodness and mercy shall follow me all the days of my life: and I will dwell in the house of the Lord forever."*

David knew that God always had his back, He knew the Lord was his Sheppard and that he did not have to fear because God was with him at all times. That is how we must think. Steadfast in believing that God is with us at all times. Even in the darkness of times he is that bright light that guides us. The same God that parted that red sea is the same God and he is parting the red seas in our lives. God already has a plan for whatever we are facing. Our story is already written out in the pages of the book. We are just living out the pages.

Psalm 139:13-17 says, "For you formed my inward parts; you covered me in my mother's womb. I will praise thee for I am fearfully and wonderfully made. Marvelous are thy works and that my soul knoweth right well. My substance was not hidden from thee. When I was made in secret, and curiously wrought in the lowest parts of the earth. Thine eyes did see my substance, yet being unperfect and in thy book all my members where written which in continuance were fashioned when yet there was none of them. How precious also are thy thoughts unto me o God! How great is the sum of them."

Understanding, just like a book chapter ends and a new chapter starts, all we have to do is to walk this out. Stand firm my sisters. We are going to make it.

Stop, close your eyes, take a deep breath, and see yourself crossing through the Red Sea. Hold your hand out and believe God is taking your hand and leading you through the water. Can you see Him. He is right there. Now open your eyes and rejoice in this moment. Get up and get moving. As I am writing I am believing God for you that your faith is increasing and that you can feel your strength coming back to your body. It may feel like you have been in this battle too long, but today celebrate because you are coming out ... I believe for you.

Together with my sister we will cross to the other side. We will get to our next chapter together. We can do all things because it is Christ Jesus that gives us strength.

Reflection

Reflections Of Hope

"A miracle sometimes involves a process. Ask God to add his super to your natural."

"You've got kingdom authority inside of you." (Apostle Delmarva Johnson)

"The devil can't kill what God has ordained to live."

"There is no expiration date on a call."

"God won't bless what you don't bring to Him."

"Gather up all your broken pieces and get ready to take them to the potter—and let Him put them back together. God specializes in making things brand new."

"Let Him re-make you, Re-shape you, smooth out the rough places with His hands. That pressure on the wheel you are feeling is His love building you back."

"Be confident in who God called you to be."

Don't lose hope, help is on the way—God is about to come through.

"The righteous cry out, and the Lord hears them; He delivers them from all their troubles." "The Lord is close to the brokenhearted and saves those who are crushed in spirit." The righteous person may have many troubles, but the Lord delivers him from them all. He protects al his bones, not one of them will be broken." Psalms 34:71-20

"Declare today that I'm going to see the blessings of God in the land of the living."

Come and declare this is your season.

He allows the path to be difficult because He is refining us and preparing us for our place of promise.

"Today, level up your faith. Get rid of doubt and cast your cares on Jesus."

"You will never achieve more than you believe you can."

"If God said it, you can believe it."

What you are going through is but a light affliction. It is not going to break you. It is for God's glory. The harder the fight, the greater the victory. Believe God is about to do something amazing in your life.

God is with us in the storm. And He is going to come through for you. Declare your victory! Declare you healing! Declare your freedom! Declare your authority over your life! Declare that your past will not determine your future!

God said in Jeramiah 32:27; "I am the God of all flesh. Is there anything too hard for me." So, you must hang in there like a good soldier and declare the word of the God over your situation.

Believe God that you are built for the battle.

-Compiled by Sucora Williams Anderson

About the Author

Evangelist O'Keiya Dinnall is a resident of Brunswick County, where she has spent her entire life cultivating deep roots within the community. Over the course of 27 years, she has stood by the side of her God sent husband Fray Dinnall embracing the joys and challenges of marriage. As a loving mother of two and a doting grandmother to three grandchildren, family holds a central place in O'Keiya's heart. However, O'Keiya's journey has not been without its share of struggles. Through experiences of abuse and trauma, she has forged a path forward with resilience and the guiding hand of faith. With a compassion for those who have endured similar hardships, O'Keiya's heart is committed to offering support and empowerment to women overcoming adversity. Armed with a degree in biblical studies and theology, and a master's degree in divinity, O'Keiya finds solace and purpose in sharing the transformative power of God's word with the lost and broken. She is the visionary and founder of a Nonprofit outreach "With My Sister Inc. "established in 2018. She is a licensed and ordained minister and serves as the youth pastor at Embracing Christ Fellowship church. Her passion for ministry extends beyond the pulpit, as she actively serves as the Re-entry Coordinator for the Ray House for Women, a division of Christian Recovery Center Inc. In this role, O'Keiya facilitates the transition of women back into society, empowering them to reclaim their independence and rebuild their lives on a foundation of hope and resilience. Driven by her faith and compassion, O'Keiya continues to make an impact within her community, one life at a time.

Printed in the USA
CPSIA information can be obtained
at www.ICGtesting.com
LVHW050957100924
790558LV00014B/318